KRGV

V

THE DOOR

BOOKS BY MARGARET ATWOOD

FICTION
The Edible Woman
Surfacing
Lady Oracle
Dancing Girls
Life Before Man
Bodily Harm
Murder in the Dark
Bluebeard's Egg
The Handmaid's Tale
Cat's Eye
Wilderness Tips
Good Bones
The Robber Bride
Alias Grace
The Blind Assassin
Good Bones and Simple Murders
Oryx and Crake
The Penelopiad
The Tent
Moral Disorder

NON-FICTION
Survival: A Thematic Guide to Canadian Literature
Days of the Rebels 1815–1840
Second Words
Strange Things: The Malevolent North in Canadian Literature
Negotiating with the Dead: A Writer on Writing
Moving Targets: Writing with Intent, 1982–2004

POETRY
The Circle Game
The Animals in That Country
The Journals of Susanna Moodie
Procedures for Underground
Power Politics
You Are Happy
Selected Poems
Two-Headed Poems
True Stories
Interlunar
Selected Poems II: Poems Selected and New 1976–1986
Morning in the Burned House
The Door

MARGARET ATWOOD

—

The Door

LIBRARY AND ARCHIVES CANADA CATALOGUING IN PUBLICATION

Atwood, Margaret, 1939–
The door : poems / Margaret Atwood.

ISBN 978-0-7710-0880-1

I. Title.

PS8501.T86D66 2007   C811'.54   C2007-900764-3

We acknowledge the financial support of the Government of Canada through the
Book Publishing Industry Development Program and that of the Government of
Ontario through the Ontario Media Development Corporation's Ontario Book
Initiative. We further acknowledge the support of the Canada Council for the
Arts and the Ontario Arts Council for our publishing program.

Typeset in Van Dijck by M&S, Toronto
Printed and bound in Canada

ANCIENT FOREST
FRIENDLY

McClelland & Stewart Ltd.
75 Sherbourne Street
Toronto, Ontario
M5A 2P9
www.mcclelland.com

3 4 5   11 10 09 08 07

FOR MY FAMILY

—

I

—

GASOLINE

Shivering in the almost-drizzle
inside the wooden outboard,
nose over gunwale,
I watched it drip and spread
on the sheenless water:

the brightest thing in wartime,
a slick of rainbow,
ephemeral as insect wings,
green, blue, red, and pink,
my shimmering private sideshow.

Was this my best toy, then?
This toxic smudge, this overspill
from a sloppy gascan filled
with essence of danger?

I knew that it was poison,
its beauty an illusion:
I could spell *flammable*.

But still, I loved the smell:
so alien, a whiff
of starstuff.

I would have liked to drink it,
inhale its iridescence.
As if I could.
That's how gods lived: *as if*.

EUROPE ON $5 A DAY

Sunrise. The thin pocked sheets
are being washed. The city's old,
but new to me, and therefore
strange, and therefore fresh.
Everything's clear, but flat —
even the oculist's dingy eyes,
even the butcher's, with its painted horse,
its trays of watery entrails
and slabs of darkening flesh.

I walk along,
looking at everything equally.
I've got all I own in this bag.

I've cut myself off.
I can feel the place
where I used to be attached.
It's raw, as when you grate
your finger. It's a shredded mess
of images. It hurts.
But where exactly on me
is this torn-off stem?
Now here, now there.

Meanwhile the other girl,
the one with the memory,
is coming nearer and nearer.
She's catching up to me,
trailing behind her, like red smoke,
the rope we share.

This is the year of sorting,
of throwing out, of giving back,
of sifting through the heaps, the piles,
the drifts, the dunes, the sediments,

or less poetically, the shelves, the trunks,
the closets, boxes, corners
in the cellar, nooks and cupboards —

the junk, in other words,
that's blown in here, or else been saved,
or else has eddied, or been thrown
my way by unseen waves.

For instance: two thick layers
of blank glass jars that once held jam
we made in those evaporated
summers; a frugal slew
of plastic bags; a cracked maroon umbrella
so prized when new;

a chocolate box with crayon ends
stored up for phantom children;
shoes with the grimy marks
of toes that once were mine.
Photos of boys whose names are lost
(posing so jauntily in front of chrome-
trimmed cars), many of them
dead now, the others old —

everything speckled, faded, jumbled
together like – let's say – this bowl
of miscellaneous pebbles gathered
age after age on beaches now
eroded or misplaced, but scooped up then
and fingered for their beauty,
and pocketed, space-time crystals
lifted from once indelible days.

Resurrecting the dolls' house
lying dormant for fifteen years,
left behind by its owner,
we unswaddle the wrapped furniture,
wake up the family:
mother and father; a boy and girl
in sailor suits; a frilly baby;
grandmother and grandfather,
their white hair dusty –
all as it should be,
except for an extra, diminutive father
with suave spats and a moustache:
maybe a wicked uncle
who will creep around at night
and molest the children.

No – let's make him good!
Perhaps a butler, or cook.
He's the one who can potter over
the real iron stove, with lids,
pour water into the hip bath,
dish up the dubious meals
made of baked Fimo:
the gruesome omelette, the meatballs,
the cake, lopsided and purple.

Now picture the house all neatly arranged,
the way it used to be:
Dad snoozing in his rocker,

tiny newspaper in hand,
Mother supine with her knitting,
the needles as big as her legs,
grandparents conked out on the best bed,
the butler counting up eggs and apples,
the kids at the dinky piano.

Stand back: now it's a home.
It glows from within.
The welcome mat says *Welcome*.
Still, it makes us anxious —
anxieties of the nest.
How can we keep it safe?
There's so much to defend.
There might be illnesses, or shouting,
or a dead turtle.
There might be nightmares.
Lucky if it's just the toast
that catches fire.

Madelaine is only three
but she knows already
the baby's too big for the carriage.
No matter how hard you cram it in,
one day, when it should be sleeping,
it will slip through a blank in your memory
and get away.

BLACKIE IN ANTARCTICA

My sister phones long distance:
Blackie's been put down.
Incurable illness. Gauntness and suffering.
General heartbreak.
I thought you'd want to bury him,
she says, in tears.
So I wrapped him in red silk
and put him in the freezer.

Oh Blackie, named bluntly
and without artifice by small girls,
black cat leaping from roof to roof
in doll's bonnet and pinafore,
Oh sly fur-faced idol
who endured worship and mauling,
often without scratching,
Oh yowling moon-
addict, devious foundling,
neurotic astrologer
who predicted disaster
by then creating it,

Oh midnight-coloured
faithful companion of midnight,
Oh pillow hog,
with your breath of raw liver,
where are you now?

Beside the frozen hamburger
and chicken wings: a paradise
for carnivores. Lying in red silk
and state, like Pharaoh
in a white metallic temple, or
a thin-boned Antarctic
explorer in a gelid parka,
one who didn't make it. Or
(let's face it) a package
of fish. I hope nobody
en route to dinner
unwraps you by mistake.

What an affront, to be equated
with meat! Catlike, you hated
being ridiculous. You hungered
for justice, at set hours and in the form
of sliced beef stew
with gravy.
You wanted what
was coming to you.
    (Death
is, though. Ridiculous. And coming to you.
For us too.
Justice is what we'll turn into.
Then there's mercy.)

MOURNING FOR CATS

We get too sentimental
over dead animals.
We turn maudlin.
But only those with fur,
only those who look like us,
at least a little.

Those with big eyes,
eyes that face front.
Those with smallish noses
or modest beaks.

No one laments a spider.
Nor a crab.
Hookworms rate no wailing.
Fish neither.
Baby seals make the grade,
and dogs, and sometimes owls.
Cats almost always.

Do we think they are like dead children?
Do we think they are a part of us,
the animal soul
stashed somewhere near the heart,
fuzzy and trusting,
and vital and on the prowl,
and brutal towards other forms of life,
and happy most of the time,
and also stupid?

(Why almost always cats? Why do dead cats
call up such ludicrous tears?
Why such deep mourning?
Because we can no longer
see in the dark without them?
Because we're cold
without their fur? Because we've lost
our hidden second skin,
the one we'd change into
when we wanted to have fun,
when we wanted to kill things
without a second thought,
when we wanted to shed the dull thick weight
of being human?)

JANUARY

Crisp scent of white narcissus:
January, and full snow.
So cold the pipes freeze.
The front steps are slick and treacherous;
at night the house crackles.

You came in and out at will,
but this time of year you'd stay indoors,
plump in your undertaker's fur,
dreaming of sunlight,
dreaming of murdered sparrows,
black cat who's no longer there.

If only you could find your way
from the river of chill flowers,
the forest of nothing to eat,
back through the ice window,
back through the locked door of air.

BUTTERFLY

My father, ninety years ago,
at the age of – my guess – ten,
walked three miles through the forest
on his way to school

along the sedgy wetfoot shore
of the brimming eel-filled rush-fringed
peat-brown river,
leaving a trail of jittering blackflies,
his hands already broad and deft
at the ends of his fraying sleeves.

Along this path he noticed
everything: mushroom and scat, wildbloom,
snail and iris, clubmoss, fern and cone.

It must have been an endless
breathing in: between
the wish to know and the need to praise
there was no seam.

One day he saw a drenched log floating
heavily downstream,
and on it a butterfly, blue as eyes.
This was the moment (I later heard)
that shot him off on his tangent

into the abstruse world
of microscopes and numbers,
lapel pins, cars, and wanderings,

away from the ten square miles
of logged-out bushlots
he never named as poverty,
and the brown meandering river
he was always in some way after that
trying in vain to get back to.

My mother dwindles and dwindles
and lives and lives.
Her strong heart drives her
as heedless as an engine
through one night after another.
Everyone says *This can't go on,*
but it does.
It's like watching somebody drown.

If she were a boat, you'd say
the moon shines through her ribs
and no one's steering,
yet she can't be said to be drifting;
somebody's in there.
Her blind eyes light her way.

Outside, in her derelict garden,
the weeds grow almost audibly:
nightshade, goldenrod, thistle.
Each time I hack them down
another wave spills forward,
up towards her window.
They batter the brick wall slowly,

muffle border and walkway,
slurring her edges.
Her old order of words
collapses in on itself.
Today, after weeks of silence,

she made a sentence:
I don't think so.

I hold her hand, I whisper,
Hello, hello.
If I said *Goodbye* instead,
if I said, *Let go,*
what would she do?

But I can't say it.
I promised to see this through,
whatever that may mean.
What can I possibly tell her?
I'm here.
I'm here.

CRICKETS

September. Wild aster. Fox grapes,
tiny and bitter,
the indigo taste of winter
already blooming inside them.

The house is invaded by crickets,
they've come inside for the warmth.
They creep into the stove
and behind the refrigerator,
make sorties across the floor,
singing to one another:
Here, here, here, here.
We step on them by mistake,
or pick them up, dozens of them,
dozens of wriggling black consciences,
and throw them out the door.

There's nothing for them to eat,
not with us. No more harvests or granaries,
only tables and chairs.
We have become too affluent.
Inside, they'd die of hunger.
Wait, wait, wait, wait, they say. They fear
they'll freeze. Under the broom
their dark armour crackles.

The ant and the grasshopper have
their places in our bestiaries:
the first stows wealth, the second

spends. We hold the middle ground, approve
the ant (head), love
the (heart) grasshopper,
emulate both: why choose?
We hoard and fiddle.

As for the crickets, they've
been censored. We have
no crickets on our hearths. We have no hearths.

Nevertheless, they wake us
at cold midnight,
small timid voices we can't locate,
small watches ticking away,
cheap ones; small tin mementoes:
late, late, late, late,
somewhere in the bedsheets,
in the bedsprings, in the ear,
the hordes of the starved dead
come back as our heartbeats.

II

THE POET HAS COME BACK . . .

The poet has come back to being a poet
after decades of being virtuous instead.

Can't you be both?
No. Not in public.

You could, once,
back when God was still thundering vengeance

and liked the scent of blood,
and hadn't got around to slippery forgiveness.

Then you could scatter incense and praise,
and wear your snake necklace,

and hymn the crushed skulls of your enemies
to a pious chorus.

No deferential smiling, no baking of cookies,
no *I'm a nice person really.*

Welcome back, my dear.
Time to resume our vigil,

time to unlock the cellar door,
time to remind ourselves

that the god of poets has two hands:
the dextrous, the sinister.

HEART

Some people sell their blood. You sell your heart.
It was either that or the soul.
The hard part is getting the damn thing out.
A kind of twisting motion, like shucking an oyster,
your spine a wrist,
and then, hup! it's in your mouth.
You turn yourself partially inside out
like a sea anemone coughing a pebble.
There's a broken plop, the racket
of fish guts into a pail,
and there it is, a huge glistening deep-red clot
of the still-alive past, whole on the plate.

It gets passed around. It's slithery. It gets dropped,
but also tasted. Too coarse, says one. Too salty.
Too sour, says another, making a face.
Each one is an instant gourmet,
and you stand listening to all this
in the corner, like a newly hired waiter,
your diffident, skilful hand on the wound hidden
deep in your shirt and chest,
shyly, heartless.

Your children cut their hands on glass
by reaching through the mirror
where the beloved one was hiding.

You weren't expecting this:
you thought they wanted happiness,
not laceration.

You thought the happiness
would appear simply, without effort
or any kind of work,

like a bird call
or a pathside flower
or a school of silvery fish

but now they've cut themselves
on love, and cry in secret,
and your own hands go numb

because there's nothing you can do,
because you didn't tell them not to
because you didn't think

you needed to
and now there's all this broken glass
and your children stand red-handed

still clutching at moons and echoes
and emptiness and shadow,
the way you did.

Time for gardening again; for poetry; for arms
up to the elbows in leftover
deluge, hands in the dirt, groping around
among the rootlets, bulbs, lost marbles, blind
snouts of worms, cat droppings, your own future
bones, whatever's down there
supercharged, a dim glint in the darkness.
When you stand on bare earth in your bare feet
and the lightning whips through you, two ways
at once, they say you are grounded,
and that's what poetry is: a hot wire.
You might as well stick a fork
in a wall socket. So don't think it's just about flowers.
Though it is, in a way.
You spent this morning among the bloodsucking
perennials, the billowing peonies,
the lilies building to outburst,
the leaves of the foxgloves gleaming like hammered
copper, the static crackling among the spiny columbines.
Scissors, portentous trowel, the wheelbarrow
yellow and inert, the grassblades
whispering like ions. You think it wasn't all working
up to something? You ought to have worn rubber
gloves. Thunder budding in the spires of lupins,
their clumps and updrafts, pollen and resurrection
unfolding from each restless nest
of petals. Your arms hum, the hair
stands up on them; just one touch and you're struck.
It's too late now, the earth splits open,

the dead rise, purblind and stumbling
in the clashing of last-day daily
sunlight, furred angels crawl
all over you like swarming bees, the maple
trees above you shed their deafening keys
to heaven, your exploding
syllables litter the lawn.

So here we are again, my dear,
on the same shore we set out from
years ago, when we were promising,
but minus – now – a lot of hair,
or fur or feathers, whatever.
I like the bifocals. They make you look
even more like an owl than you are.
I suppose we've both come far. But

how far are we truly, from where we started,
under the fresh-laid moon, when we plotted
to astound? When we thought
something of meaning could still be done
by singing, or won, like trophies.
I took the fences, you the treetops, where we
hooted and yowled our carnivorous
fervid hearts out, and see,
we did get prizes: there they are,
a scroll, a gold watch, and a kissoff
handshake from the stand-in
for the Muse, who couldn't come herself,
but sent regrets. Now we can say

flattering things about each other
on dust jackets. Whatever
made us think we could change the world?
Us and our clever punct-
uation marks. A machine-gun, now –

that would be different. No more unct-
uous adjectives. Cut straight to the verb.
Ars longa, mors brevissima. The life
of poetry breeds the lust
for action, of the most ordinary
sort. Whacking the heads off dandelions,
or bats or bureaucrats,
smashing car windows. Though

at least we've been tolerated,
or even celebrated — which meant
a brief caper in the transient glare
of the sawdust limelight,
and your face used later for fishwrap —
but most of the time ignored
by this crowd that has finally admitted
to itself it doesn't give
much of a fart for art,
and would rather see a good evisceration
any day. You might as well have been
a dentist, as your father hoped. You

want attention, still? Take your clothes off
at a rush-hour stoplight, howl obscenities,
or shoot someone. You'll get
your name in the paper, maybe,
for what it's worth. In any case

where do we both get off?
Is this small talent we have prized
so much, and rubbed like silver
spoons, until it shone

at least as brightly as neon, really
so much better than the ability
to win the sausage-eating contest,
or juggle six plates at once?
What's the use anyway
of calling the dead back, moving stones,
or making animals cry? I

think of you, loping along at night
to the convenience store, to buy your pint
of milk, your six medium eggs,
your head stuffed full of consonants
like lovely pebbles
you picked up on some lustrous beach
you can't remember – my feather-
headed fool, what have you got
in your almost-empty pockets
that would lure even the lowliest mugger?
Who needs your handful
of glimmering air, your foxfire, your few
underwater crystal tricks
that work only in moonlight?
Noon hits them and they fall apart,
old bones and earth, old teeth, a bundleful
of shadow. Sometimes, I know, the almost-holy
whiteness rooted in our skulls spreads out
like thistles in a vacant lot, a hot powdery
flare-up, which is not a halo
and will return at intervals
if we're grateful or else lucky, and
will end by fusing our neurons. Yet

singing's a belief
we can't give up.
Anything can become a saint
if you pray to it enough –
spaceship, teacup, wolf –
and what we want is intercession,
that iridescent ribbon
that once held song to object.
We feel everything hovering
on the verge of becoming itself:
the tree is almost a tree, the dog
pissing against it won't be a dog
unless we notice it
and call it by its name: "Here, dog."
And so we stand on balconies and rocky
hilltops, and caterwaul our best,
and the world flickers
in and out of being,
and we think it needs our permission. We

shouldn't flatter ourselves: really
it's the other way around. We're at
the mercy of any stray
rabid mongrel or thrown stone or cancerous
ray, or our own
bodies: we were born with mortality's
hook in us, and year by year it drags us
where we're going: down. But

surely there is still
a job to be done by us, at least
time to be passed; for instance, we could

celebrate inner beauty. Gardens.
Love and desire. Lust. Children. Social justice
of various kinds. Include fear and war.
Describe what it is to be tired. Now
we're getting there. But this is much
too pessimistic! Hey, we've got
each other, and a roof, and regular
breakfasts! Cream and mice! For

our sort, elsewhere, it's often worse:
a heaved boot, poisoned meat, or dragged
by the wings or tail off to some wall
or trench and forced to kneel
and have your brains blown out, splattering all over
that Nature we folks are so keen on –
in the company of a million others,
let it be said –
and in the name of what? What noun?
What god or state? The world becomes
one huge deep vowel of horror,
while behind those mildewed flags, the slogans
that always rhyme with *dead*,
sit a few old guys making money. So

honestly. Who wants to hear it?
Last time I did that number, honey,
the audience was squirrels.
But I don't need to tell you.
The worst is, now we're respectable.
We're in anthologies. We're taught in schools,
with cleaned-up biographies and skewed photos.
We're part of the mug show now.

In ten years, you'll be on a stamp,
where anyone at all can lick you. Ah

well, my dear, our leaky cardboard
gondola has brought us this far,
us and our paper guitar.
No longer semi-immortal, but moulting owl
and arthritic pussycat, we row
out past the last protecting
sandbar, towards the salty
open sea, the dogs'-head gate,
and after that, oblivion.
But sing on, sing
on, someone may still be listening
besides me. The fish for instance.
Anyway, my dearest one,
we still have the moon.

THE POETS HANG ON

The poets hang on.
It's hard to get rid of them,
though lord knows it's been tried.
We pass them on the road
standing there with their begging bowls,
an ancient custom.
Nothing in those now
but dried flies and bad pennies.
They stare straight ahead.
Are they dead, or what?
Yet they have the irritating look
of those who know more than we do.

More of what?
What is it they claim to know?
Spit it out, we hiss at them.
Say it plain!
If you try for a simple answer,
that's when they pretend to be crazy,
or else drunk, or else poor.
They put those costumes on
some time ago,
those black sweaters, those tatters;
now they can't get them off.
And they're having trouble with their teeth.
That's one of their burdens.
They could use some dental work.

They're having trouble with their wings, as well.
We're not getting much from them
in the flight department these days.
No more soaring, no radiance,
no skylarking.
What the hell are they paid for?
(Suppose they are paid.)
They can't get off the ground,
them and their muddy feathers.
If they fly, it's downwards,
into the damp grey earth.

Go away, we say —
and take your boring sadness.
You're not wanted here.
You've forgotten how to tell us
how sublime we are.
How love is the answer:
we always liked that one.
You've forgotten how to kiss up.
You're not wise any more.
You've lost your splendour.

But the poets hang on.
They're nothing if not tenacious.
They can't sing, they can't fly.
They only hop and croak
and bash themselves against the air
as if in cages,
and tell the odd tired joke.
When asked about it, they say

they speak what they must.
Cripes, they're pretentious.

They know something, though.
They do know something.
Something they're whispering,
something we can't quite hear.
Is it about sex?
Is it about dust?
Is it about fear?

POETRY READING

Watching the poet – the well-known poet –
ransacking his innards, laying out
his full stock of destructive thoughts
and shamefaced lusts,
his stale hatreds, his weak but shrill ambitions,
you don't know whether to be scornful or grateful:
he's doing our confessions for us.

He's encased in a soft pullover,
defiantly not black, but pale yellow
like a cream sorbet, the colour
you buy for toddlers when you don't wish to look sexist,
and his face with its worried forehead
floats against the dark stage background,
the features a little indistinct
like the sun through mist,

and you understand how this face was, once,
when he was an anxious little boy
balanced on tiptoe, staring into the mirror
and asking, *Why can't I be good?*
and later, *Are these my real parents?*
and later still, *Why does love hurt so much?*
and even later, *Who causes wars?*

You want to take him in your arms
and tell him a bunch of lies.
Normal folks don't ask those things,
you might say. *Let's have sex instead.*

You know that women stupider than you
have proposed this remedy for all ills
of the mind and spirit. You've vowed never to do that,
so you're making a big exception here.

But he would only reply,
I've told you about my scabs and compulsions,
my grubby torments, my lack of dignity –
I'd just get you dirty.
Why bother with me?

At which you'd answer:
No one made you do this,
this fooling with syllables,
this rolling naked in thistles
and sticking your tongue onto nails.
You could have been a bricklayer.
You could have been a dentist.
Hard-shelled. Impervious.

But that's useless. Lots of bricklayers
have blown their heads off with shotguns
out of blank despair. With dentists the rate's higher.
Maybe it's *instead of*, this poetry.
Maybe the string of words
that's coming out of him now like a peeled vein
is all that's holding him tethered
to a few square feet of this earth.

So you keep on watching, as he flays himself
in an ecstasy of self-reproach;
he's down to his underwear now,

the hair shirt, the chains —
N.B., these are metaphors —
and you see that after all
there's a cold craft to it, as with beadwork
or gutting a mackerel.
There are techniques, or gimmicks.

But just as you're feeling tricked
his voice cuts abruptly. There's a small nod,
and a smile, and a pause,
and you feel your own intake of breath
like a fist of air slamming into you,
and you join the applause.

She squats, bare feet
splayed out, not
graceful; skirt tucked around ankles.

Her face is lined and cracked.
She looks old,
older than anything.

She's probably thirty.
Her hands also are lined and cracked
and awkward. Her hair concealed.

She prints with a stick, laboriously
in the wet grey dirt,
frowning with anxiety.

Great big letters.
There. It's finished.
Her first word so far.

She never thought she could do this.
Not her.
This was for others.

She looks up, smiles
as if apologizing,
but she's not. Not this time. She did it right.

What does the mud say?
Her name. We can't read it.
But we can guess. Look at her face:

Joyful Flower? A Radiant One? Sun on Water?

The singer of owls wandered off into the darkness.
Once more he had not won a prize.
It was like that at school.
He preferred dim corners, camouflaged himself
with the hair and ears of the others,
and thought about long vowels, and hunger,
and the bitterness of deep snow.
Such moods do not attract glitter.

What is it about me? he asked the shadows.
By this time they were shadows of trees.
Why have I wasted my lifeline?
I opened myself to your silences.
I allowed ruthlessness
and feathers to possess me.
I swallowed mice.
Now, when I'm at the end, and emptied
of words, and breathless,
you didn't help me.

Wait, said the owl soundlessly.
Among us there are no prices.
You sang out of necessity,
as I do. You sang for me,
and my thicket, my moon, my lake.
Our song is a night song.
Few are awake.

III

—

TEN O'CLOCK NEWS

The shot bird topples from the air,
the others note it:
they need to know what's going on.
Tree leaves rustle, deer twitch their tails, rabbits
swivel their ears.
The grass-eaters crouch, the scavengers
lick their teeth.
Spilled life does not appall them.

What alerts us? What are we feeding on?
We take everything in,
one wound after another.
Rubble rubble, say the guns.
Our faces gleam in the glassy flicker,
the night rises like smoke.

Oh hide your eyes —
better to sit in a muffled room,
doors locked, appliances unplugged,
with nothing but the photo view
of Niagara Falls you bought last summer —
all that soothing water
like warm green toffee flowing
in slow motion over a cliff,

trying not to see the weak swimmer,
or the two children in their yellow boat.

THE WEATHER

We used to watch the birds;
now we watch the weather.
White clouds, downy as pillows,
grey ones like giant thumbs,
dark ones, fat with doom.

Once, we didn't bother.
We had umbrellas, and rooms.
But while we were looking elsewhere,
at wars or other diversions,
the weather crept up behind us
like a snake or thug or panther
and then cut loose.

Why were we so careless?
we ask ourselves, as the weather billows
over the horizon, green
and yellow, thickening itself
with sand and body parts and broken
chairs and shouts.
In its wake we shrivel or drown.

How can we cram it back
into the sack or bottle
where it used to be so small?
Who let it out?

If the weather's listening at all
it's not to us.

Is it our fault?
Did we cause this wreckage by breathing?
All we wanted was a happy life,
and for things to go on as they used to.

The wind falls. There's a hush,
a half-hour silence in heaven.
Then here comes the weather
– again, again –
one huge relentless blare,
trampling everything down,
singeing the air.

It's blind and deaf and stupendous,
and has no mind of its own.
Or does it? What if it does?
Suppose you were to pray to it,
what would you say?

It's autumn. The nuts patter down.
Beechnuts, acorns, black walnuts —
tree orphans thrown to the ground
in their hard garments.

Don't go in there,
into the faded orange wood —
it's filled with angry old men
sneaking around in camouflage gear
pretending no one can see them.

Some of them aren't even old,
they just have arthritic foreheads,
or else they're drunk,
but something's got to suffer
for their grudges, their obscure sorrows:
the more blown-up flesh, the better.

They'll shoot at any sign of movement —
your dog, your cat, you.
They'll say you were a fox or skunk,
or duck, or pheasant. Maybe a deer.

They aren't hunters, these men.
They have none of the patience of hunters,
none of the remorse.
They're certain they own everything.
A hunter knows he borrows.

I remember the long hours
crouching in the high marsh grasses –
the low sky empty, the water silent,
the hushed colours of distant trees –
waiting for the rush of wings,
half-hoping nothing would happen.

BEAR LAMENT

You once believed if you could only
crawl inside a bear, its fat and fur,
lick with its stubby tongue, take on
its ancient shape, its big paw
big paw big paw big paw
heavy-footed plod that keeps
the worldwide earthwork solid, this would

save you, in a crisis. Let you enter
into its cold wise ice bear secret
house, as in old stories. In a desperate
pinch. That it would share
its furry winter dreamtime, insulate
you anyway from all the sharp and lethal
shrapnel in the air, and then the other million
cuts and words and fumes
and viruses and blades. But no,

not any more. I saw a bear last year,
against the sky, a white one,
rearing up with something of its former
heft. But it was thin as ribs
and growing thinner. Sniffing the brand-new
absences of rightful food
it tastes as ripped-out barren space
erased of meaning. So, scant

comfort there.

Oh bear, what now?
And will the ground
still hold? And how
much longer?

ICE PALACE

Another ice palace. Another demi-
paradise where all desires
are named and thus created,
and then almost satisfied. *Hotel*
might be an accurate label.

Not made of glass and marzipan
and steel, and jewel-toned water,
and opal gelatin that glows
like phosphorescent deep-sea fish, as
you might think at first. But no,

it's only dreams, it's only
clouds of breath formed into
words: the heavenly bed, the all-
you-can-eat breakfast. Invisible hands
bring food, smooth down

the sheets, turn on the lights,
cause violins to lullaby
the sugared air, clean out the wad of hair
you left in the porcelain shower,
and place a rose on your pillow

when you're not there. Where
is the fearful beast who runs the show
and longs for kisses?
Where are the bodies that were once
attached to all those hands?

Backstage it's always carnage.
Red petals on the floor.
You hope they're petals. Don't unlock
the one forbidden door,
the one inscribed

Staff Only. Do not look
in the last and smallest room, oh
dearest, do not look.

SECRECY

Secrecy flows through you,
a different kind of blood.
It's as if you've eaten it
like a bad candy,
taken it into your mouth,
let it melt sweetly on your tongue,
then allowed it to slide down your throat
like the reverse of uttering,
a word dissolved
into its glottals and sibilants,
a slow intake of breath –

and now it's in you, secrecy.
Ancient and vicious, luscious
as dark velvet.
It blooms in you,
a poppy made of ink.

You can think of nothing else.
Once you have it, you want more.
What power it gives you!
Power of knowing without being known,
power of the stone door,
power of the iron veil,
power of the crushed fingers,
power of the drowned bones
crying out from the bottom of the well.

THE LAST RATIONAL MAN

In the reign of Caligula

The last rational man takes his old seat in the Senate.
He's not sure why he's still here.
He must be on some list or other.
Last year there were many more like him,
but they've been picked off one by one.
He bathes daily, and practises slow breathing
and the doctrines of Stoicism.
Lose your calm, he reminds himself,
and you will lose everything.
Nevertheless he's getting tired.
The effort of saying nothing is wearing him down.
The others in their rich men's outfits
banter carefully, sticking to topics
that grow fewer in number; even the weather
is perilous, the sun too,
since the Emperor claims to control the one
and to be the other.

Here he comes now, with his chittering retinue
of paid retainers twitchy with bonhomie;
he's gilded and bright as a chariot in false taste,
and just returned from a fresh triumph.
With a grin he lifts his gleaming finger:
baskets of shells cascade onto the floor,
and the room stinks of dead molluscs.
Look, says the Emperor, *it's treasure!*
By the power of my supreme divinity

I've defeated the King of the Sea!
His eyes hold the malicious glitter
of a madman who's telling a lie,
and knows it, and dares contradiction.

The others cheer. The last rational man
forces himself to cheer also.
The Emperor's gaze is boring a hole
through the bellowing air straight towards him.
Then they lead in the Emperor's horse,
wreathed in garlands like a belly dancer.
I'm making him a Senator!
trills the Emperor. *Greet your new brother!*

The last rational man finds himself rising.
As he opens his mouth he can see
the red bathwater, his own slit wrists,
his house robbed, his sons headless.
That's only a horse, he says.
The words hang there
hopelessly, like the banners of a city
already defeated, given over to pillagers.
In what way, thinks the last rational man,
can such a place be said, still, to exist?

Silence crystallizes
around his head like a halo of ice.
He stands there.
No one looks at him except the Emperor,
who smiles at him with something almost like pity.

WHITE COTTON T-SHIRT

White cotton T-shirt: an innocent garment then.
It made its way to us from the war, but we didn't know that.
For us it was the vestment of summer,
whiter than white, shining with whiteness
because it had been washed in blood, but we didn't know that,
and in the cropped sleeve, rolled up tightly
into a cuff, were tucked the cigarettes,
also white within their packet, also innocent,
as were white panties, white convertibles,
white-blond brush-cuts,
and the white, white teeth of the lilting smiles
of the young men.

Ignorance makes all things clean.
Our knowledge weighs us down.
We want it gone

so we can put on our white T-shirts
and drive once more through the early dawn
streets with the names we never could
pronounce, but it didn't matter,
over the broken glass and bricks, passing
the wary impoverished faces,
the grins filled with blackening teeth,
the starving dogs and stick children
and the slackened bundles of clothing
that once held men,

enjoying the rush of morning air
on our clean, tanned skins,
and the white, white flowers we hold out in our fists,
believing – still – that they are flowers of peace.

WAR PHOTO

The dead woman thrown down on the dusty road
is very beautiful.
One leg extended, the other flexed, foot pointed
towards the knee, the arm flung overhead, the hand
relaxed into a lovely gesture
a dancer might well study for years
and never attain.
Her purple robe is shaped
as if it's fluttering;
her head is turned away.

There are other dead people scattered around
like trees blown over,
left in the wake of frightened men
battering their way to some huge purpose
they can't now exactly remember,

But it's this beautiful woman who holds me,
dancing there on the ground
with such perfection.

Oh dead beautiful woman, if anyone
had the power to wrench me through despair
and arid helplessness
into the heart of prayer,
it would be you –

Instead I'll make for you
the only thing I can:

although I'll never know your name,
I won't ever forget you.
Look: on the dusty ground
under my hand, on this cheap grey paper,
I'm placing a small stone, here:
                              o

Even if you had remained alive,
we would never have spoken.
Suppose we'd shared a road,
a car, a bench, a table —

Maybe you would have offered me
a piece of bread, a slice of lemon.
Or else there would have been suspicion,
or fear, or nothing.

Now though it seems I am asking
and you are answering:

Why is the tree dying?
  It is dying for lack of truth.

Who has blocked up the wells of truth?
  Those with the guns.

What if they kill all those with no guns?
  Then they will kill one another.

When will there be compassion?
  When the dead tree flowers.

When will the dead tree flower?
  When you take my hand.

This is the kind of thing
that goes on only in poetry.
You are right to be suspicious of me:
I can't speak your absence for you.

(Why is it then I can hear you so clearly?)

Nobody cares who wins wars.
They care at the moment:
they like the parades, the cheering;
but after that, winning diminishes.
A silver cup on the mantle
engraved with some year or other;
a hoard of buttons cut from corpses
as souvenirs; a shameful thing
you did in white-hot anger shoved
back out of sight.
Bad dreams, a bit of loot.
There's not much to say about it.

That was a fine time, you think.
I've never felt more alive.
Nonetheless, victory puzzles you.
Some days you forget where you've put it,
though younger men make speeches about it
as if they had been there too.

Of course it's better to win
than not. Who wouldn't prefer it?

Losing, though. That's different.
Defeat grows like a mutant vegetable,
swelling with the unsaid.
It's always with you, spreading underground,
feeding on what's gone missing:
your son, your sister, your father's house,

the life you should have had.
It's never in the past, defeat.
It soaks into the present,
it stains even the morning sun
the colour of burnt earth.

At last it breaks the surface.
It bursts. It bursts into song.
Long songs, you understand.
They go on and on.

THE VALLEY OF THE HERETICS

(Luberon Valley, Provence)

This is the valley of the heretics: once far
away from everything, now overrun
by the forces of invasion, ourselves included.
In our metal shell we're off to see the sights:
a green river; a hundred-year-old fountain
with a sly-eyed naked girl reclined in stone
underpinning the town's notables; the rows
of flapping scarves and aprons; trestle tables
with bric-a-brac – chess sets and salt cellars
left over from vanished households, plaster
cicadas labelled "artisan," probably made in Taiwan.

We're not there yet. We fight our way through the air
while the reed beds and bushes thrash as if pounded.
The dry wind hurtles down on us; torn plastic
bags like ectoplasmic birds flitter and stream,
and gusts buffet the sign showing a big red blood drop
with white gloves and a grin, and the other poster,
a girl in underwear licking her lips and smirking.
These would have been sinister magic
once, anywhere icons were rife, but especially here
between the secretive mountains, this harsh
rock-strewn place infected with goats and sorcery.

As we rush through clouds of the scouring dust
that puffs into the car and powders our hair,
fine lines race across our faces

like speeded-up films of neglected frescoes.
The heretics, holed up in their hilltop towns,
taught that the body was trash,
the earth was made by a lesser, malignant god —
for which thoughts they were set on fire, and burned
in anguish. We wish not to believe them
but on windy days like this we breathe them in
with unease, a sense of foreboding:
their ashes are everywhere.

Here's Joan in her penitential bedsheet,
peeled of her armour, hair shorn,
wrapped round with string
like a boned rolled leg of lamb,

topped with a hat that looks like paper,
newspaper at that, but without the print,
a conical dunce cap.
Everything pale, hands, bare feet,
thin vestment, drained and blank,
white as the centre of a flare:
foreknowledge does that.

Some cleric putting a match to her.
Neither of them looks happy about it.
Once lit, she'll burn like a book,
like a book that was never finished,
like a locked-up library.

Her two left-handed angels
and the ardent catchwords
they whispered into her ear –
Courage! Forward! King!
will burn as well.
Their voices will shrivel and blow away
in a scrawl of ash,

charred scraps of a dirty joke
in the long and dissolute narrative
people keep telling themselves about God,

and the watchers in the square will cheer,
incinerating her with their eyes,
since everyone likes a good bonfire
and a nice cry, some time afterwards.

It's you reading her now,
reading the Book of Joan.
What do you make of her?
Joan, the cocksure messenger,
or lunatic, or glassy sphere
containing a pure, terse chapter
of a story with both ends missing?

You'll patch up some translation,
you and your desk-lamp lightbulb,
you and your white-hot stare.

THE HURT CHILD

The hurt child will bite you.
The hurt child will turn
into a fearsome creature
and bite you where you stand.

The hurt child will grow a skin
over the wound you have given it
– or not given, because the wound
is not a gift, a gift is accepted
freely, and the child had no choice.

It will grow a skin over the wound,
the hoarded wound, the heirloom wound
you have pried out of yourself like a bullet
and implanted in its flesh –
a skin a hide a pelt
a scalded rind,
and sharp fish teeth
like a warped baby's –
and it will bite you

and you will cry foul
as is your habit
and there will be a fight
because you'll take the fight out of the box
labelled *Fights* you keep so carefully stored
against emergencies, and this is one,

and the hurt child will lose the fight
and it will go lurching off
into the suburbs, and it will cause
panic in drugstores and havoc
among the barbecues
and they will say *Help help a monster*
and it will get into the news

and it will be hunted
with dogs, and it will leave a trail
of hair, fur, scales, and baby teeth, and tears
from where it has been ripped
by broken glass and such

and it will hide in culverts
in toolsheds, under shrubs,
licking its wound, its rage,
the rage you gave it
and it will drag itself to the well

the lake the stream the reservoir
because it is thirsty
because it is monstrous
with its raging thirst
which looks like spines all over it

and the dogs and the hunters will find it
and it will stand at bay
and howl about injustices
and it will be torn open
and they will eat its heart

and everyone will cheer,
Thank god that's over!

And its blood will seep into the water
and you will drink it every day.

THEY GIVE EVIDENCE

(After a room-sized installation by Dadang Christanto, 1996)

They give evidence
in an empty room
sixteen of them, eight men, eight women,
four rows of four,
unlucky number.

They are all bald,
they are all naked,
they all have wide shoulders,
huge hands, strong legs, huge feet.

Their skin is greyish white,
greyish brown,
mineral colours, dusty and scarred
as if they have been buried;
as if they have been buried a long time
and secretly dug up, like ancient sculptures
guarding the bones of kings;
as if they have been dead.

But they are not dead exactly.
Their mouths are open, although there are no tongues;
their eyes are open, although there are no eyes;
they have the spaces for tongues and eyes,
empty spaces;
they are speaking and looking
with this emptiness they carry.

They carry emptiness,
they carry empty clothing.
Coloured and patterned, not faded,
red yellow blue, shirts blouses trousers,
moulded in the shapes of bodies,
the bodies cloth once held.
Men and women, and children
four children, five
children, six,
it's hard to tell.

Those who are naked carry the clothes
that never have been theirs.
They carry the clothes gently
as if the clothes are asleep,
as if the vanished bodies inside the clothes are sleeping,
the bodies of air.
Gently, they hold out the stiff empty clothing
like frozen garlands now, like offerings.
Like unfortunate flowers.

They speak words, I think.
They testify.
They name names.
That's what you'd assume.

Or perhaps it's a chant,
a prayer a question.
Perhaps they are singing praises.

To whom are they chanting and praying?
Who are they questioning?

The wall they face is blank.
Whose praises do they sing?

Perhaps they are angels
of a new kind, bald and eyeless
and without wings.
Angels are messengers.
Perhaps they bring a message.
The messages of angels
are seldom lucky.

(What are the names?)

IV

—

Enough of these discouragements,
you said. Enough gnawed skulls.
Why all these red wet tickets
to the pain theatricals?
Why these boxfuls of ruin?
Whole big-block warehouses full.
Why can't you tell about flowers?

But I did tell, I answer.
Petal by petal, snowdrop and rose
unfolding in season, I told them all –
the leaf, the stem, the intricate bloom –
I praised each one in its turn.
I told about sunsets, as well,
and silvery dawns, and noons.
I told about young men
playing their flutes beside pools
and young girls dancing.
I raised up fountains, golden pears:
such gentle miracles.

You didn't want them,
these pastel flavours.
You were bored by them.

You wanted the hard news,
the blows of hammers,
bodies slammed through the air.
You wanted weaponry,

the glare of sun on metal,
the cities toppled, the dust ascending,
the leaden thud of judgment.
You wanted fire.

Despite my singed feathers
and this tattered scroll I haul around,
I'm not an angel.
I'm only a shadow,
the shadow of your desires.
I'm only a granter of wishes.
Now you have yours.

POSSIBLE ACTIVITIES

You could sit on your chair and pick over the language
as if it were a bowl of peas.
A lot of people do that.
It might be instructive.
You don't even need the chair,
you could juggle plates of air.

You could poke sticks through the chain-link fence
at your brain, which you keep locked up in there,
which crouches and sulks like an old tortoise,
and glares out at you, sluggish and eyeless.
You could tease it that way,
make it blunder and think,
and emit a croaking sound
you could call truth.
A harmless activity,
sort of like knitting,
until you go too far with it
and they bring out the nooses and matches.

Or you could do something else.
Something more sociable.
More group-oriented.
A lot of people do that too.
They like the crowds and the screaming,
they like the adrenalin.

Hunker down. Get a blackout curtain.
Pretend you're not home.

Pretend you're deaf and dumb.
Look: pitchforks and torches!
Judging from old pictures,
things could get worse.

QUESTIONING THE DEAD

Go to the mouth of a cave,
dig a trench, slit the throat
of an animal, pour out the blood.

Or sit in a chair
with others, at a round table
in a darkened room.
Close your eyes, hold hands.

These techniques might be called
the heroic and the mezzotint.
We aren't sure we believe in either,

or in the dead, when they do appear,
smelling like damp hair,
flickering like faulty toasters,
rustling their tissue paper
faces, their sibilants, their fissures,
trailing their fraudulent gauze.

Their voices are dry as lentils
falling into a glass jar.
Why can't they speak up clearly
instead of mumbling about keys and numbers,
and stairs, they mention stairs . . .

Why do we keep pestering them?
Why do we insist they love us?
What did we want to ask them
anyway? Nothing they wish to tell.

Or stand by a well or pool
and drop in a pebble.
The sound you hear is the question
you should have asked.

Also the answer.

THE NATURE OF GOTHIC

I show you a girl running at night
among trees that do not love her
and the shadows of many fathers

without paths, without even
torn bread or white stones
under a moon that says nothing to her.
I mean it says: *Nothing.*

There is a man nearby
who claims he is a lover
but smells of plunder.
How many times will he have to tell her
to kill herself before she does?

It's no use to say
to this girl: You are well cared for.
Here is a safe room, here
is food and everything you need.

She cannot see what you see.
The darkness washes towards her
like an avalanche. Like falling.
She would like to step forward into it
as if it were not a vacancy
but a destination,
leaving her body pulled off
and crumpled behind her like a sleeve.

I am the old woman
found always in stories like this one,
who says, *Go back, my dear.*

Back is into the cellar
where the worst is,
where the others are,
where you can see
what you would look like dead
and who wants it.

Then you will be free
to choose. To make
your way.

THE LINE: FIVE VARIATIONS

I)

The line is a white thread,
or so we're told. You fasten
one end of it to a tree or bed
or threshold, and footfall
by footfall, you unscroll
this line behind you

as you step into the cave to meet
whatever's in there —

the ill will of the universe,
a shucked lover,
the core of your own head —
compacted fire,
monstrous, horned, sacred.

You hold your breath,
one heartbite
after another.
Tastes familiar.

II)

The line is a lifeline,
it leads you out again
to the profane. To vegetables

and sex, and eggs
and bacon. Fodder. Wallow. Time
as generally understood.
Breakfast, lunch, dinner,
architecture,
all those things
that won't miss you
when you're elsewhere.
There. Feel better?

III)

Reverse the field and the line is black,
the cavern a whiteout.
A blank, a snow.
The monster not a burning coal,
but ice-furred shadow.

Where does that get you?
Out of the body, onto the page,
the line the net
in which you tangle God –
O, paper wendigo –

in the midst of his blizzard,
in the midst of his avalanche
of *nihilo*,
going about his business,
wringing stars out of zero.

iv)

The line's for fishing.

You hook the big one, haul him in.
You net his flounderings.
You write him down, the Word
made word. You've earthed him,
all his acts and sufferings. He seeps
out of your fingers now, like wine-dark blood
set free.
    Oh oh. You've cut his noose,
you've let him loose. He's gone
with the spiralling wind, he's roaring
from the mountaintop:
Here comes Time!
Yum! Yum! Yum! Yum!

Now we'll have massacres.

v)

That was some line
you fed us! What a bad story!

Keep your hands to yourself
next time! Don't touch that paper!
We don't need no war-surplus history
tall tales around this place. We don't
need more *And then.*

But you never would listen.
Think you're some kind of poet.
Now look what you've done,
you and your damn line –
mucking around with creation.

You just had to fool with it.
You just can't leave it alone.

ANOTHER VISIT TO THE ORACLE

1) *Another visit to the oracle*

There's so much I could tell you
if I felt like it. Which I do less and less.
I used to verbalize a mile a minute,
but I've had to give it up. It's
too hard to turn the calories into words,
as you'll find out too if you live
long enough. If you live as long as me.
So I've had to edit. I've taken up
aphorism. Cryptic, they say.
Soon I'll get everything down to one word.
All crammed in there, very
condensed you understand, like an
extremely small black star. Like a black
hole. Like a dense potential. Like the letter A.
You see what I mean about cryptic.
I could go on like this for hours. Weeks months
years centuries millennia. Could and did.
It was my vocation, after all. My
fate. That, and the lack of accurate
translation. Want to know your future?
But you'd rather have a happy story any
day. Or so you say.

2) *Prophecy*

The future will be both better than the past
and worse.

What future?
Your future,
which is implied in many futures.
What past?
Your past,
which is touched by many pasts.
Both your future and your past are in your head,
because where else could they be?
And your head is in the present, since
by the time you hear this, "your head" –
the one I just mentioned –
is already in the past,
which doesn't exist, except
in your head as I'm telling you this.
Prophecy is therefore easy.
All I have to do
is be present in my head,
which contains your head.
I can walk around in there
as if in a cave,
a well-lit cave.
I can look at any feature.
This is one method.
It only seems like magic.

3) *They used to ask me . . .*

They used to ask me all kinds of questions:
Will I get a good husband
Will I be rich
Will the baby recover

and so on.
Now it's only the one thing:
Is there no hope?
They ask that over and over.
Though the sky is as blue as ever
the flowers as flowery,
they stand there slack-mouthed
arms hanging useless
as if the earth is about to crumble,
as if there is no safe refuge.
Of course, I say.
I hate to disappoint.
Of course there's hope.
It's over there in that well.
There's an endless supply.
Bend over the rim, you'll see.
Down there.
It looks like silver.
It looks like you
with the sun behind your head
as if your brain is burning.
The face dark and without features.
But that's a trick of the light.
That's hope.
It's in the future tense.
Don't be deceived.

4) *Don't be deceived . . .*

Don't be deceived.
What a thing to say.

As if there's no conspiracy.
Relax, the lightbulbs are singing.
It will soon be all right,
hum the wires.
You'd think it was spring,
so many tunes on the loose
bursting with love, and all of it
mechanical.
Deception is the air we breathe,
we couldn't live without it.
Don't you want things nice?
Don't you want to have fun?
Don't you want your dinner?
Clap your hands and wish very hard.
That's what we're eating:
Wish food.

5) *Wish food*

Wish food lies on the plate.
It twitches. It's still alive.
You wouldn't want a dead wish.

Those go bad very fast.
But if wishes were fishes
we'd soon be out of luck.

Eat, eat, the body says:
Here comes starvation
blowing towards you like a dry wind.
Nobody has a plan.

You'll need that fat,
all those fat wishes,
those fat dreams you ate.

Start working on your burrow,
the one you'll crawl into
so you can hibernate.

Call upon your inner bear,
it's in there.

6) *Why should I tell you anything true?*

1)

Why should I tell you anything true?
Why should I tell you anything?
You're not paying me.
I don't do this for money.

Hold out your hand,
your empty hand.
I see.
If I told you what you hold
in the lines in your hand
which as I said is empty,
is full of emptiness,
you'd be annoyed. Oh surely
not, you'd say. You're far too
dismal. Too severe.

I'm doing this to help you.
What would you prefer?
You'd like me to amuse you?
Do some jigs, or pranks?
I lack the airiness,
I lack the feathers.
That's not what I do.

What I do: I see
in darkness. I see
darkness. I see you.

II)

I see you,
in darkness, walking.
I see your hurrying feet.
This is where you'll be
at the end of all the sunsets,
all the banquets.

Behind you there's a tunnel
with a life in it.
Your former life,
your life of silks and gardens.
Colours flickering.
The city is in flames,

it's as I said:
time to get out
with what you're carrying.

Forget the jewellery,
forget the lovers you once had.
Don't hesitate.
You can find other bangles.

Ahead of you there's what?
Is it a river?
The water slides like oil,
soundless and without fish.
A mute beach.

This is where I'm handy:
I've been here
in some form or another.
I'll help you to the edge,
I'll see you over.
I know who to bribe.
Don't be afraid.

III)

Don't be afraid.
A boat will be provided.
After the boat has foundered,
after you've reached the shore
despite the foundering boat,
after you've met whoever's waiting,
who loves you (possibly),
after you've entered
the part that I can't see,

I'll tell your story –
your story that was once so graceful
but now is dark.
That's what I do:
I tell dark stories
before and after they come true.

V

—

BOAT SONG

There's pushing and scrabbling,
not nearly enough lifeboats:
that much is obvious;

so why not spend the last few moments
practising our modest art
as we have always done,

creating a pool of possibly false comfort
in the midst of tragedy?
There's something to be said for it.

Picture us then in the ship's orchestra.
We all stay in our places,
tootling and strumming and marking time

with our workaday instruments
as the shouts and boots trample past.
Some have jumped; their furs and desperations

weigh them down. Clawed hands reach up through the ice.
What are we playing? Is it a waltz?
There's too much uproar

for the others to make it out clearly,
or else they're too far away —
an upbeat foxtrot, a sugary old hymn?

Whatever it is, that's us with the violins
as the lights fade and the great ship slides down
and the water closes in.

DUTIFUL

How did I get so dutiful? Was I always that way?
Going around as a child with a small broom and dustpan,
sweeping up dirt I didn't make,
or out into the yard with a stunted rake,
weeding the gardens of others
– the dirt blew back, the weeds flourished, despite my efforts –
and all the while with a frown of disapproval
for other people's fecklessness, and my own slavery.
I didn't perform these duties willingly.
I wanted to be on the river, or dancing,
but something had me by the back of the neck.
That's me too, years later, a purple-eyed wreck,
because whatever had to be finished wasn't, and I stayed late,
grumpy as a snake, on too much coffee,
and further on still, those groups composed of mutterings
and scoldings, and the set-piece exhortation:
Somebody ought to do something!
That was my hand shooting up.

But I've resigned. I've ditched the grip of my echo.
I've decided to wear sunglasses, and a necklace
adorned with the gold word NO,
and eat flowers I didn't grow.
Still, why do I feel so responsible
for the wailing from shattered houses,
for birth defects and unjust wars,
and the soft, unbearable sadness
filtering down from distant stars?

I used to have helpfulness tacked onto me
like a fake string tail on a mangled dog.
Wag, wag, wag went my nerveless appendage:
If I give you something, will you like me?

Watch me make you happy!
Here's a dry stick for you!
I fetched it off the ash heap.
Here's a dead bird.
There! Aren't I good?

Here's a gnawed bone,
it's my own,
I took it out of my arm.
Here's my heart, in a little pile of vomit.

Was it my fault you were angered
by the world news? That you bad-mouthed God
and banking, and in addition the weather?
That you sulked all day and were vicious
to your mirror, and also
to the girls at checkout counters?
That you thought sex was a mess?

I did my best. Wag, wag
went my tail of string.
Have some drool and mud!
Admire my goodwill! It clings
to the soles of your boots

like soft pink melting jelly.
Here, take it with you!
Take everything, and then I'm free;
I can run away. I'm blameless.
You can have the string tail, too.

STEALING THE HUMMINGBIRD CUP

Mexico. For Mónica Lavin

Once I had a greed for the world.
I wanted to steal things,
I wanted to steal a lot of things.
In recent years, very few.

But today I felt larceny
creeping back into my fingers:
I wanted to steal the hummingbird cup.
If you had a large hand

and you put thumb to index,
that would be the circumference.
If you had a small eye,
the hummingbird would be smaller.

The cup is dark red,
the colour of dried blood,
with a painted feather, or else a wind,
or else a word.

The hummingbird is bright blue.
It perches on the rim
and dips its beak down into the cup,
drinking from what used to be there.

Who made it?
Who was it made for?

Who poured what into it?
With what pleasure?

If only I could steal this cup –
break the glass case, make off with it!
This cup full of happiness
that looks like air,
or spent breath, or shadows
on a day with no sun,
that looks like nothing,
that looks like time,

that looks like whatever you want.

ONE DAY YOU WILL REACH . . .

One day you will reach a bend in your life.
Time will curve like a wind
and after that the young
will no longer be afraid of you
the way they ought to be,

the way they were when you were minus fifty
and had a glare like winter,
and kept men's souls in cough syrup bottles
and could cause dogs to burst into flames.

Instead of fear, you'll be handed
a kind of dutiful respect
that isn't really serious
and will find yourself an object
of secret jocularity
like a preposterous expensive hat.
The glittering eyes of the old aren't gay

or if gay, they have the gaiety
of things that have no power.
Wallpaper with pink flowers.
Buds in bud vases. Butterflies
drunk on fermenting pears.
Drunks in the gutter.

Drunks in the gutter singing –
I forgot to add that.

Disturbed earth: some plants sprout quickly in it.
Sow thistles come to mind.
After you've wrenched them out
they'll snake back underground
and thrust their fleshy prickled snouts in
where you intended hostas.

Hawkweed will do that. Purslane. Purple vetch.
Marginals, hugging ditches,
flagrant with seed,
strewing their paupers' bouquets.

Why is it you reject them,
them and their tangled harmonies
and raffish madrigals?
Because they thwart your will.

I feel the same about them:
I hack and dig,
I stomp their pods and stems,
I slash and crush them. Still,

suppose I make a comeback –
a transmutation, say –
once I've been spaded under?
Some quirky growth or ambush?

Don't search the perennial border:
look for me in disturbed earth.

REINDEER MOSS ON GRANITE

This is a tiny language,
smaller than Gallic;
when you have your boots on
you scarcely see it.

A dry scorched dialect
with many words for holding on,
and with grey branches
like an old tree's, brittle and leafless.

In the rain they go leathery,
then sly, like rubber.
They send up their little mouths
on stems, red-lipped and round,

each one pronouncing the same syllable,
o, o, o, like the dumbfounded
eyes of minnows.
Thousands of spores, of rumours

infiltrating the fissures,
moving unnoticed into
the ponderous *is* of the boulder,
breaking down rock.

Off we go, unsteadily down the gangway,
bundled up in our fleecy layers,
mittened like infants, breasting – as they
once said – the icy waves
in our inner tube of a boat,
so full of pills we rattle.

We're what the French politely call
the Third Age: One and Two behind us, Four
still tactfully not mentioned, though
it looms. It's the one after.
Meanwhile, we scream full throttle
as the spray hits us,
delighted to be off the hook.
Not responsible.

Aaju is one of our minders –
she's got her sealskin parka on
for the camera folk, toting her bear gun.
She gives us a strict look, sideways:
she's seen too many like us
to find us truly droll.
Herding us will be like herding
lemmings. We'll wander off.
Plus, we don't listen.

We've bumbled ashore now. Time for lessons.
Jane's up today. She says:
When you see a creek like this one,

flowing into a bay,
and there's flat land for a tent,
and a view of the sea, for hunting,
and berry bushes, a hillside full,
you know there must have been people.

And sure enough, see here:
a ring of stones, a fox trap,
and farther on, a grave,
thick slabs to keep out the animals.
They like it when you visit them,
says Aaju. *Just say hello.*

So we lie down on the soft moss, gaze up
at the sky marbled with cloud
and a raven circling, and it's total peace
among the voices that do not speak,

except we can't stay here:
we need to do more real life,
see the thing through. So back we amble
in our clumsy boots and Gortex windgear,
trundling over the boulders
like huge old children called back to school.

Aaju's perched on a distant hill
to keep us harm-free.
She stands on one foot, lifts her arms,
a silent message:
Hello! I'm here!
    Here is where I am.
I stand on one foot, too.

You heard the man you love
talking to himself in the next room.
He didn't know you were listening.
You put your ear against the wall
but you couldn't catch the words,
only a kind of rumbling.
Was he angry? Was he swearing?
Or was it some kind of commentary
like a long obscure footnote on a page of poetry?
Or was he trying to find something he'd lost,
such as the car keys?
Then suddenly he began to sing.
You were startled
because this was a new thing,
but you didn't open the door, you didn't go in,
and he kept on singing, in his deep voice, off-key,
a purple-green monotone, dense and heathery.
He wasn't singing for you, or about you.
He had some other source of joy,
nothing to do with you at all —
he was an unknown man, singing in his own room, alone.
Why did you feel so hurt then, and so curious,
and also happy,
and also set free?

AT BRUTE POINT

The old people descend the hill in slow motion.
It's a windy hill,
a hill of treacheries and pebbles,
and twisted ankles.

One has a stick, one not.
Their clothing is bizarre,
though wash and wear.

Foot over foot they go,
down the eroded slope,
flapping like sails.
They want to get down to the ocean,
and they accomplish this.

(Could it be that we are the old people
already?
Surely not.
Not with such hats.)

We may have been here before;
at least it looks familiar,
but we are drawn to hills like these,
remote, bleak, old history,
nothing but stones.

Down by the tidal pool
there are two plastic bottles
a few small molluscs.

One person pees in a corner
out of the sun,
the other, not.

At this point, once, there might have been sex
with the waves rampaging in
as if in films.

But we stay fully clothed,
talk about rocks:
how did it get this way, the mix
of igneous and sandstone?
There's mica too, that glitter.

It's not sad. It's bright
and clear.
See how spryly we climb back up,
one claw and then the other.

THE DOOR

The door swings open,
you look in.
It's dark in there,
most likely spiders:
nothing you want.
You feel scared.
The door swings closed.

The full moon shines,
it's full of delicious juice;
you buy a purse,
the dance is nice.
The door opens
and swings closed so quickly
you don't notice.

The sun comes out,
you have swift breakfasts
with your husband, who is still thin;
you wash the dishes,
you love your children,
you read a book,
you go to the movies.
It rains moderately.

The door swings open,
you look in:
why does this keep happening now?
Is there a secret?
The door swings closed.

The snow falls,
you clear the walk while breathing heavily;
it's not as easy as once.
Your children telephone sometimes.
The roof needs fixing.
You keep yourself busy.
The spring arrives.

The door swings open:
it's dark in there,
with many steps going down.
But what is that shining?
Is it water?
The door swings closed.

The dog has died.
This happened before.
You got another;
not this time though.
Where is your husband?
You gave up the garden.
It became too much.
At night there are blankets;
nonetheless you are wakeful.

The door swings open:
O god of hinges,
god of long voyages,
you have kept faith.
It's dark in there.
You confide yourself to the darkness.
You step in.
The door swings closed.

Acknowledgements

Some of these poems have appeared in the following publications:

"Blackie in Antarctica": *Ontario Review* 48 (spring/summer 1998).

"Mourning for cats": *Poetry Ireland Review* (2005).

"Butterfly": *The First Man in My Life: Daughters Write About Their Fathers.* Toronto: Penguin Canada, 2007.

"My mother dwindles . . .": *Sunday Times* (U.K.), January 2007.

"Crickets": *Landfall 201* (2001); CBC's "In the Works," 1999; *Ontario Review* 49 (fall/winter 1998).

"The poet has come back . . .": www.thewordlounge.com; Ali Smith, ed. *The Reader.* London: Constable & Robinson, 2006.

"Heart": *Landfall 201* (2001); *Ontario Review* 49 (fall/winter 1998); *RSA Journal (Rivista di Studi Nord-Americani)* 8–9 (1997–1998).

"Sor Juana works in the garden": *20th-Century Poetry and Poetics,* 5th ed., Toronto: Oxford University Press, 2006; trans. and pub. in Spanish *Anthology of Contemporary Poetry by Women,* American Studies Association of Italy, 1997; *Landfall 201* (2001); *Ontario Review* 48 (spring/summer 1998); *RSA Journal (Rivista di Studi Nord-Americani)* 8–9 (1997–1998).

"Owl and Pussycat, some years later": *Pretext 5* (May 2002); *Verandah* 12 (1997).

"The poets hang on": *Poetry Ireland Review* (2005).

"A poor woman learns to write": *PEN America 7* (2006).

"The singer of owls": Parliamentary Poet Laureate website, www.parl.gc.ca, August 2006.

"Secrecy": *New Yorker,* 28 August 2006.

"They give evidence": *This Magazine,* November/December 2006; trans. and pub. in Latvian *Karogs* (2007).

"Questioning the dead": *Landfall 201* (2001); *Ontario Review* 48 (spring / summer 1998); *RSA Journal (Rivista di Studi Nord-Americani)* 8–9 (1997–1998).

"The nature of Gothic": *Ontario Review* 48 (spring/summer 1998); *RSA Journal (Rivista di Studi Nord-Americani)* 8–9 (1997–1998).

"Another visit to the Oracle": *Exile* (spring 2007).

"String tail": *Poetry Ireland Review* (2005).

"Reindeer moss on granite": *Lichen and Reindeer Moss on Granite: A Broadside Poem*. Port Townsend, WA: Copper Canyon Press, 2000; trans. and pub. in Latvian *Karogs* (2007).